Ways Into RE

Symbols of Faith

Louise Spilsbury

W

FRANKLIN WATTS

LONDON • SYDNEY

Published by Franklin Watts
338 Euston Road
London NW1 3BH

Franklin Watts Australia
Level 17/207 Kent Street
Sydney NSW 2000

ISBN 978 1 4451 3042 2
Dewey classification number: 203.7

Series editor: Julia Bird
Art director: Jonathan Hair
Design: Shobha Mucha
Consultant: Joyce Mackley, RE Advisor at RE Today

A CIP catalogue record for this book is available
from the British Library.

Picture credits:

Athar Akram/Ark/Alamy: 20t; Ark Religion/Alamy: 9tr;
Paula Bronstein/Getty Images: front cover t; Kristian Buns/Alamy: 17; Ranjan Chari
istockphoto: 27tl; Mike Cherim/istockphoto: 20b; Robert Churchill/istockphoto:
21tr; Distinctive Image/Shutterstock: 12t; Louise Batalla Duran/Alamy: 21cl;
Chris Fairclough/Watts Archive: 22t; Tim Gainey/Alamy: 7t; Andreas Gradin/istockphoto: 6cr; Ralf
Grosch/Shutterstock: 6t; GW Images/Shutterstock: 18; Image Source/Alamy: 14t;
Victor de Jesus/Alamy: 26; David Kerkoff/istockphoto: 8b; John Warburton-Lee/Alamy: 11; Liz
Leyden/istockphoto: 23; Olivier Martel/Corbis: 24t; Tjasa Maticic/Shutterstock: 7b;
Andrew McConnell/Alamy: 8tl; Phillip Meyer/Shutterstock: 27br;
Indranil Mukherjee/Getty Images: 19; Christine Osborne/World Religions PL/
Alamy: 3, 13; Regien Paassen/Shutterstock: 25; Panaspics/Shutterstock: 14b;
Photohamster/istockphoto: 6bl; Jack Puccio/istockphoto: 16;
Johan Ramberg/istockphoto: 27bl; Homer Sykes/Alamy: 22b;
Con Tanasiuk/Alamy: 12b; Tova Teitelbaum/istockphoto: 27tr;
Wilson Valentin/istockphoto: 8tr; Susan Vogel/Getty Images: front cover bl;
Winterling/istockphoto: front cover br; World Religions PL: 10, 15, 24b;
Yuka Zubritsky/istockphoto: 9l.

Printed in Malaysia

Franklin Watts is a division of Hachette Children's Books,
an Hachette UK company.
www.hachette.co.uk

Contents

What are symbols?

Symbols are pictures or objects that have a special meaning. They are used to stand for or represent something else.

A red traffic light symbol says stop.

This symbol shows that something can be recycled.

This symbol warns drivers that the road ahead is slippery.

Talk about...
...what symbols you know. Think about the ones you see every day, and how they help people.

Religion is often about things we cannot see, like God. Symbols describe ideas and help to explain things we cannot see.

The symbol for Hinduism is Om. It represents God and all that He created.

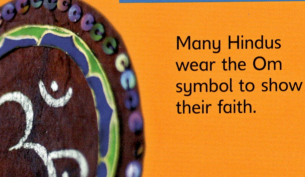

Many Hindus wear the Om symbol to show their faith.

What other symbols are used for different religions? Think about which ones you know, then turn the page to find out.

Symbols for religions

The cross is a symbol for the Christian faith. Jesus died on a cross. It reminds Christians that Jesus died and rose again.

A star and crescent moon is a symbol for Islam. Some people believe that the five points of the star stand for the five pillars of Islam. These are five rules that Muslims live by.

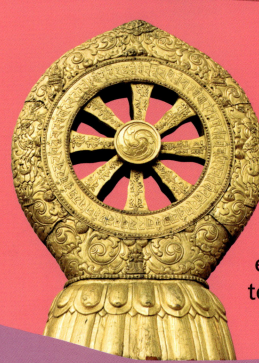

The symbol for Buddhism is a wheel with eight spokes. This represents Buddha's eight teachings.

The circle in the Sikh khanda symbol has no end. It shows that God is always there. The swords represent truth and fighting for what is right.

The Star of David is a symbol of the Jewish faith. It is on the flag of Israel. Many Jews believe that David was the best king Israel ever had. He ruled over 2,500 years ago.

Think about...
...designing a symbol for your family. You could use:
• shapes • patterns • colours
• pictures • numbers

Stories

Holy books contain stories about a religion. Symbols are important in religious stories.

In the story of Noah's Ark, Noah's boat saves his family and animals from a huge flood sent by God. After a year, a dove brings Noah an olive branch to show God's judgement is over. The dove and the olive branch are symbols of peace and hope.

Sometimes a whole story is a symbol that teaches people an important lesson.

The story of the monkey-god Hanuman and the god Rama is in a Hindu holy book. Hanuman's monkey army wins a fierce fight against a demon called Ravana to help rescue Rama's wife. The story is a symbol for the way good wins over evil.

What other stories can you think of that work as a symbol to teach a lesson?

Actions

Symbols can also be things people say or do, like when we wave to mean goodbye.

When Muslims pray, they follow a pattern of special movements such as bowing and kneeling down. These show that Muslims are humble and that they worship their God, Allah.

Some Christians make the sign of the cross in front of their body before they pray. This shows their belief in God.

Sikhs wave a whisk called a chauri over the Sikh holy book, the Guru Granth Sahib, as they read it. This is a symbol of their respect for their holy book.

Think about...
... the actions or gestures you make every day. Keep a record of them and what they mean. You could include:
•waving •clapping •hugging
•shaking hands •shrugging your shoulders

Objects

Tefillin

Religious people may wear, hold or carry objects that have special meaning.

A tefillin is a small box that contains an important Jewish prayer. Some Jews wear a tefillin when they pray to remind them of God's teachings.

A Christian bishop is in charge of many of the churches in an area. His stick is shaped like a shepherd's crook to show that he is like a shepherd, looking after his flock.

The five Ks are like a Sikh uniform which some Sikhs are proud to wear to show what they believe. The five different Ks all represent different things.

Kesh: uncut hair (under turban) shows they trust God

Kirpan: sword to remind them to stand up for what is right

Kachera: short trousers, remind them of Sikhs in the past who were soldiers

Kangha: small comb reminds Sikhs to keep hair and lives organised

Kara: bracelet, circle reminds that God has no end and is everlasting

Think about...
... what other symbolic objects people have. You could include: •wedding rings •badges •souvenirs •trophies •certificates

Foods

Symbolic foods are often used to remember special events.

At the festival of Passover, the foods on a Seder plate remind Jews that their people escaped slavery in Egypt long ago.

Parsley dipped in salt water: symbols of the tears of the slaves

Egg: represents spring and new life

Bitter lettuce: symbol of the bitterness of being a slave

Lamb bone: symbol of sacrifices made the Jewish Temple

Horseradish root: also represents the bitterness of being a slave

Fruit, spice and nut mix: symbol of the mortar slaves used to make bricks

Why do you think it is important for Jews to remember this difficult time in their history?

At a special service called Communion, Christians are given bread and wine. This reminds them of the last meal Jesus ate with his friends before he died on the cross.

Think about...

...what special foods you would choose to eat to remember home if you were far away. What memories or special events would the meal remind you of?

Sounds

Sounds can have special meanings.
Some sounds are made with instruments.

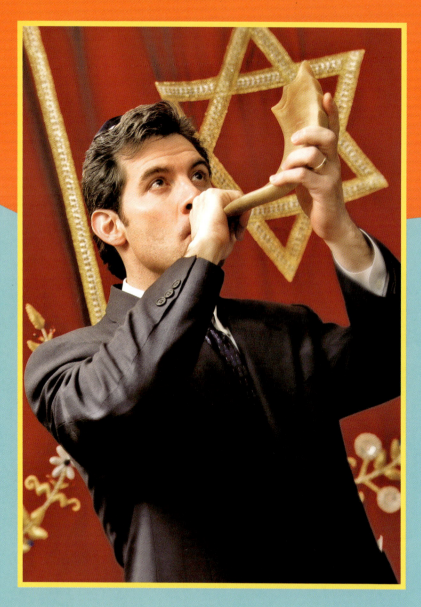

At the Jewish New Year festival, the shofar horn is blown. It tells people it is time to show they are sorry for any bad things they did in the previous year.

What sounds have meaning for you?
What does the school bell tell you?

Some sounds are made with the human voice.

Hindus chant the word 'Om' at the start and the end of most prayers. This is the sound of the symbol that represents God's creation of the whole world.

Think about...
... the way religious symbols affect different senses, like sight and hearing. Why do people use symbols that appeal to all of the senses?

Colours

Colours can be symbols, too. Colours have different meanings for different religions.

Muslims wear simple white clothes when they go on a pilgrimage to Makkah. This is a way of showing that all Muslims are equal before Allah.

The shawl that some Jewish men wear for prayer is mainly white. This colour represents Earth. It is trimmed with blue. This stands for heaven.

Some Buddhist monks wear orange or yellow robes. This is because yellow is seen to be healing and warm, like the Sun.

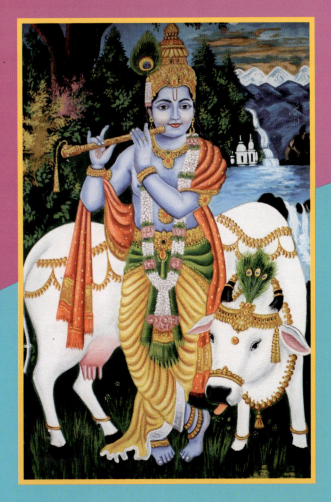

Krishna is a Hindu god with blue skin. Blue is the colour of the sky and ocean. It suggests that like the sky and oceans, God is endless and all around us.

Think about...
... the different meanings that colours can have. What does it mean when someone is feeling blue, for example? Think of meanings for these colours:
- white
- yellow
- green
- black

Light

Light is a symbol that is used in several religions.

Divali is the Hindu festival of lights. Diva lamps are lit to chase away darkness. This is a symbol that God can chase away evil in the world.

At a Christingle service, Christians hold a candle in an orange. The orange is a symbol of the world. The candle is a symbol that God helps people see the right way to live.

At the festival of Hanukkah, Jews remember winning back the city of Jerusalem long ago.

In their temple, a miracle happened. An oil lamp burned for eight days without oil. Jews light eight candles on a Hanukkiah candlestick as a symbol of God's power.

Talk about...
...when do you use light as a symbol?
What do candles on a birthday cake represent?

Another important religious symbol is water. Why do you think this is? Turn the page to find out.

Water

Christians are baptised when they join the Church. Water is a symbol of washing away their sins to show that they are ready to start a new life with God.

When Muslims wash before entering a mosque, it is not because they are dirty. It is a symbol of washing away wrongdoing. It shows that they are ready to pray.

To Hindus, the River Ganges is a holy river. Many Hindus make a pilgrimage to bathe in its waters. Doing this is a symbol for washing away bad thoughts, actions or feelings.

Think about...
... when you wash carefully and why. What does washing do? How do you feel when you have washed?

A symbol safari

Go on a symbol safari! When you go out, hunt for religious symbols. Draw or download and print off the Internet the different symbols you see. Make a note of where you saw them.

Look for...
... religious symbols in all kinds of places:
- buildings
- clothes
- badges
- jewellery
- statues
- flags
- head coverings

Can you guess the meanings of your symbols before checking if you are right?

Make a display with your symbols collection. Add captions saying where you found them.

Star of David
Religion: Jewish
Location: Necklace

Om symbol
Religion: Hindu
Location: Temple

Cross
Religion: Christian
Location: Church window

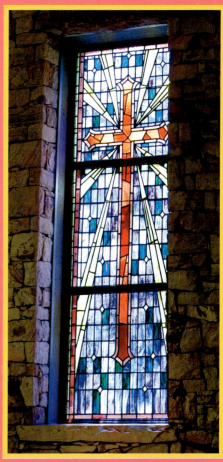

Star and crescent moon
Religion: Islam
Location: Turkey flag

The six main faiths

The world's six main faiths are Hinduism, Christianity, Buddhism, Islam, Judaism and Sikhism. Each of the six main faiths have different beliefs:

Hindus believe there is one God that can take different forms. Hindus worship these different gods and goddesses.

Christians believe there is one God who has three parts: The Father, the Son and the Holy Spirit. Jesus is the son of God and was sent to Earth to save people.

Buddhists do not worship a God. They follow the teachings of a man called Buddha and try to live in the way he taught.

Muslims follow the religion of Islam. They follow five rules known as the Five Pillars: to believe in one God – Allah, to pray five times a day, to fast during the month of Ramadan, to give money to the poor and to go on pilgrimage to Makkah.

Jewish people believe that there is one God who made everything and that they should follow Jewish law.

Sikhs believe that there is one God who made everything. They follow the teachings of ten Gurus (teachers) who told people what God wanted.

Useful words

Faith – another word for religion.

Holy – something that is especially important to a religion.

Miracle – an act or event that could not normally happen and that people believe is caused by God.

Pilgrimage – a journey to a holy place for religious reasons.

Prayer – words people say to speak to, give thanks to or ask for help from God. The Lord's prayer is an important Christian prayer.

Religion – belief in a God or gods. Islam and Christianity are two religions.

Sacrifice – usually means when an animal is killed as an offering to a god.

Sin – when someone does something that breaks a religious law.

Symbol – a picture, word or number that represents something else. A cross is a symbol that represents the Christian Church.

Worship – to show respect or love for God or gods. Some people worship by praying and singing.

Index

About this book

Ways into RE is designed to develop children's knowledge of the world's main religions and to help them respect different religions, beliefs, values and traditions and understand how they influence society and the world. This title Symbols of Faith explores what symbols are and what special symbols people use in different religions.

- The children could start by discussing what symbols are and what symbols they know. They could look at symbols on washing labels, food packages or in sport to introduce the idea that you need to know something about many symbols to understand what they mean.

- When looking at stories (pages 10–11), children could look at symbols used in religious and non-religious stories, such as rocks, light, and darkness and talk about the way that symbols help to say things or describe feelings that may be hard to put into words. Within these discussions you could also introduce non-literal sayings such as 'you're driving me up the wall'; 'it's raining cats and dogs'; 'sorry, I must fly'.

- When talking about colours as symbols, you could encourage the children to think of other times colours are used in daily life and in religions. For example, green is used to mean 'go' in traffic lights and white dresses are often worn in Christian weddings as a symbol of purity.

- If at all possible, arrange a visit to two different places of worship to hunt for symbols. To extend this project they could discuss in more depth why religions use symbols. They could talk about the fact that Muslims do not represent God in images and discuss why Jewish people avoid writing God's name. Do people find other words or symbols to describe God because God is so holy and beyond words? When might actions/pictures/objects speak louder than words?